A Patchwork of Stories

A Patchwork of Stories

Published by Poetry Space Ltd. 2022

Patchwork featured on the cover was made by Barbara Bennett

Poetry Space Ltd. Company No. 7144469

2 North st, Beaminster, Dorset DT8 3DZ

Printed and bound in the United Kingdom

by Poetry Space Ltd

www.poetryspace.co.uk

ISBN: 978-1-909404– 49-6

A Patchwork of Stories

chaplaincy in life changing moments

by

Judy Dinnen

Contents

I introduce you to people, poems, pain and prayer.

Rainbow of truth
Christ you take care of our illness.
Wisdom of Sad
Trinity of Love

Section 9 – Invitation to play with words - *page 105*

Acrostic
Choose an interesting sentence and write from it.
Fill a leaf or cross shape with words
Choose an object to remember someone by
Tell your story
'When you listen deeply to me…'
Write a letter to someone who has helped you
Write a letter to God
Write an answer from God
What are fragile?

Section 9 – Playground - *page 109*

Space for you to play and write …

Poems give us the fuel that we so desperately need; they serve as sources of catharsis and hope; giving us permission to feel deeply and to feel together.

Amanda Gorman

Introduction

Set in the context of the work and experience of a hospital chaplain, this book offers poetry as a healing, focused means of exploring the world. I hope these poems will engage with the reader and offer insight and healing. The role of both chaplain and poet involves listening deeply; listening to words, noting both expression and body language. Both roles require appropriate response; standing alongside with empathy, understanding, and gentle love. Both roles have a spiritual dimension, opening up to life's meaning, the questions and pain of the patient. Throughout this exploration, I acknowledge that it is a great privilege to enter into people's stories and share their lives. I also echo the notion of the chaplain as servant; a phrase used recently by Revs Martin Abrams and Jan Fraser in an article in **The Church Times** (January 2021)

The stories in this book cover many decades and reference several hospitals across the UK, one in Germany and two in Tanzania. I hope it will offer a contribution to the ongoing debate about the importance and contribution of chaplaincy work and emphasise how this role addresses the 'spiritual' side of the patient, therefore complementing the physical and emotional. As I write the pandemic has changed hospital life enormously, there are constraints both on patients and staff and hospitals are under enormous pressure.

The book ends with a chapter offering prayers as a resource for the reader. An epilogue offers creative writing suggestions for the reader to use, personally or in a group.

I consider the role of the chaplain as well as the strengths that poetry has to offer. The role of poetry is to heal, allow exploration and differing perspectives. There are organisations that support and encourage this fascinating and complex process.

Henri Nouwen[1] tells a moving story of a young woman in L'Arche community who asked for a blessing – a 'real' blessing, and that turned out to mean a huge hug and some word of affirmation as to her worth. With those who have learning difficulties, touch may be particularly important, when words fail to communicate need fully.

In the world of the patient, there can also be an inner brokenness, confusion, isolation and fear. 'Two souls alas dwell in my breast apart' wrote Foust, referring to a 'schism between true essential self and apparent existential self'. The patient may have to confront the self in a new way, in a challenging new context. It may relate to a lack of preparedness for illness or death a subject Dennis Potter reflects upon as he approaches his own death. In our society we have an expectation of good health and death is not easily addressed.

During the hospital placement, I witnessed pain and anguish. I also found a place, where watching alongside patients was deeply appreciated and somehow there seemed to be a joy there; if joy can be taken as an embracing of a new depth of truth and love. The assistant chaplain preached about hope, joy and salvation in the chapel service; a message for all those patients sitting in their dressing gowns and in their wheelchairs.

Visits to two hospitals in Tanzania, describe the introduction and growth of the hospice movement in that country. The doctor involved, Dr Karilyn Collins has also taken this message to other countries in Africa and India. Visits to a hospital in Bavaria are described in an early section. Outside the Klinik is a statue of two simple figures facing each other. The sculptor, Reinhart Fuchs, tells us that it is a meeting of two people. One needs the other. Neither can live without the other. They each climb steps towards the other. The steps represent overcoming struggle. The accompanying poem speaks of the grace of attention, a gift that chaplains need. The figures are the human side of Godly grace.

Section One

Listening, watching, touching

Listening, watching or touching are all described as aspects of spirituality. Closely standing alongside the patient with focused attention; that is the role of the chaplain.

In this section there are poems about patients which express small moments of life in the hospital. They arise out of being with and listening to the patient and finding there something intense, of value which stirs the poetic response.

In this first poem I transform the experience into something more. I express empathy but interpret the moment in an imaginative way. I call the subject, Jim and, although I only have a glimpse into his life, his presence is felt. The recounting of the short episode affords gentle humour and perhaps relief, were he aware of it. Poetry can retell and must often reimagine with empathy, for the poet is the author and stands at the behest of the subject.

From my Placement journal 2005

Eucharist in the chapel

The service was delightfully idiosyncratic – a very mixed group of people – some coming in late – many not able to sing or even find their place in the books. One wandered in during the homily and muttered, then was later distressed. The informality allows for all of this, or rather, the chaplains allow for all who come, by pausing and welcoming late arrivals, and others making space for them.

The lesson (2 Corinthians) was about Paul's sufferings. I wondered if this was specially chosen as the lesson for the day. Paul spoke about God 'using' suffering to bring out gifts or as a way of finding direction.

I wondered what the 40 year old stroke survivor, Jim, was thinking. He had been hoisted out of bed and let gently down into a wheelchair. (see poem). He had been in hospital for 6 weeks and the day before his stroke he'd been at a Taizé service. What might he believe about all of this? What is his future? He has at last been able to come to a service in the chapel, whatever that implies. What must such dependence, loss of control, disappointment, challenge to identity be like for a youngish man? There was no opportunity for me to spend more time with him.

Wheels or Wings?

Rising, rising,
swinging left, then right.
Look at the white metal arm,
your mechanical god!
Its strength and power give hope of freedom.

You're a bird,
flying through the ward;
glance through the window,
at roof tops and grey sky.

You're flying towards the clouds,
up and over the huts,
over houses and streets,
over traffic queues and red lights,
over police station and parked Maria.

The sun smiles feebly at the joke.
Your dead arm curls in your lap.
Your hair does its own thing.

You're coming down,
down in your green sling,
they turn you and guide you,
calm words and humorous quips.

No, not a bird after all,
more a lift, 'ground floor please,'
going down,
down into your wheelchair;
wheels, not wings.

The nurse eases your feet into trainers.

May 2005

An everyday moment in the life of a patient is described here. We do not have a name for her, though we could call her Cynthia. The lines on the garment suggest the frame of mind, the uncertainty, and lack of control that Cynthia is experiencing. Her frown and her apology contribute to this interpretation depicted in the sweater's lines and creases.

Creases

Behind the coloured curtain,
in privacy of sorts,
she takes her pale sweater from the bed side locker;

sees its creases,
haphazard lines going nowhere,
not meant, not wanted,

a crazy map of cul de sacs,
alien territory,
labyrinth of impossibilities.
She smooths them vaguely with her hand.

She puts it on over her crumpled scar.
Her still face apologises to itself.
Her still eyes stare straight into tomorrow.
She sinks back into her chair,
shuts her eyes,
rests her head,
waits to go home.

Written during my college placement in Hereford Hospital.
2005

This poem tells the story of another small moment in hospital life. Violet sat on the chair beside her bed and, as I approached, she told me she was cold. The nurses were very busy, so I was asked to fetch a blanket for her. I took a white cellular blanket from the store and brought it to her. Placing it over her somehow felt quite special, as described in this poem.

The Blanket Prays

'I'm tired' she says 'and cold'.
Her small frame, bird like,
still, in pink frills;
eyes closed in search of sleep,
skin crumpled, chilled, arms and legs bare.

'I'm tired' she says 'and cold'.
I fetch a blanket,
unfurl it like words of prayer.
I spread its wings over her
small body, over knees and toes.

It encases her like an embrace.
It embraces her like a soft whisper;
covers her like the love of angels,
silent words of comfort and warmth.

'Thank you' she murmurs
under the soft white wings.
She closes her eyes,
finds the peace
of angel dreams.

Some years ago, I was diagnosed with breast cancer. I became very aware of my body and also became the patient, who is warmly listened to and touched by others.

From my cancer journal: -

‘My body is part of what I am, when I walk through the woods and feel fresh air on my face.
It is part of who I am, as I curl up in bed.
It is linked to the clothes I wear, the colours, style or labels.
My body is the person I see in the mirror, the person you meet in the street.’

At the start of August words failed me. I began to use drawing, colour, shape and images. I found new channels and new ways of healing. One of my drawings was of my scar (to represent operations, recovery, chemo, side effects, tedium, frustration and everything else that is part of the mix of treatment for breast cancer). Inspired by an art project described on Women's Hour, I started to decorate 'my scar' - to beautify it, to symbolise new possibilities .

Purple Smile

I took a lambent, purple pen,
drew a scar down the page,
a scar that said more than itself,
sign of cuts, drains, drugs and shock,
months of change and cloud.

I drew this scar, bold, upright,
then penned fine scrolls, leaves
and flowers, swirls that said beauty,
that lived the change from blood
to flowers, profusion of hope,
crests of tomorrow.

A knife, purple too, was engulfed
by these tendrils fine.
They said' Well done'
They said 'Yes' to tomorrow.
They danced future hope.
They acted out spring growth.
They lived a smile of purple,
which spreads from edge to edge,
proud picture of wounds' gash shining’.

In the 70s I visited a Cerebral palsy unit in South London. I was drawn to the unit by a bookby Maureen Unwin. I can't remember the title. She worked in this unit and saw with fresh insight, that the children and teenagers there were young people, not just patients. She described their patient-like routines and felt they needed more to their lives. She set up a school in the unit. I was privileged to work with Andy. Maureen had realised that he was intelligent, despite his inability to speak. So, she taught him to read. I sat with him on that short visit and helped him read. As a former infant teacher, I would expect to say 'I listened to him read' but of course he had no spoken words. So, I let him read, pointing to the words and indicate to me when he was stuck. It was an extraordinary and moving experience.

The second child in this poem was quite different. His life was limited, and Maureen was sensitive to his needs. There was to be a party on the ward. I can't remember the reason for it. Maureen knew that the party was not an easy place for Sam, so she decided that I was a calm person and Sam would appreciate sitting on my lap for the duration of the party. This again was another moving experience.

These stories show the importance not just of listening but of noticing, of being aware of all the signs of need and possibility shown by the children. By extension, such attention is a prime quality of the work of the chaplain and other health professionals. We are there to respond to their situations, to respond to their needs and to sensitively offer what they ask for or indicate that they need.

The boy with no tomorrow

They stirred with the sun,
washed, dressed, ate breakfast
in rows, said goodbye, then hello
to new staff, learnt to smile…

day followed day followed day

Then there was a party;
parents came, visitors too;

games and food, usual stuff,
but not for Andy and Sammy.

Andy with no voice was learning
to read. A visitor listened, no,
sat with him, watched his finger
move across the page, gave a word,
as his finger paused,
eyebrow raised.

The hold of his frame,
the power of his eyes told
the story of… well yes,
reading a story, grasping
the words, savouring them,
understanding them.

Andy was a real pupil,
silence overcome,
words mastered.

Then there was Sammy
the boy with no future.
games scared him.
Voices and hopscotch
bemused him,
balloons and song
worried him.

He needed a soft, warm, still lap.
the boy with no tomorrow
was lifted on to a safe lap.
Arms folded round him,
he enjoyed a calm, cosy today.

I was invited to take a creative writing workshop at the hospice. A mixture of patients and staff gathered in the day room and were ready to express their feelings and their views. I watched a middle-aged woman with long dark hair, as she wrote. She was intent on the task, quite still and clearly absorbed. Then I noticed a small tear run down her cheek. One of the exercises was to fill in the shape of a tear on the paper with words. This poem filled that shape and, as I knew the woman well, I filled it with places and activities that she would have enjoyed in past years. The fog at the end hints at the uncertain future she now faced.

Tear

It drops slowly down her
cheek,
redolent of yesterday.
Reflected in its curve,
I see hills and climbing.
I see waves
breaking on the shore.
I see sunshine.
I see fog.

It hovers on her cheek.
She wipes it away.

(Hospice, 2011)

This following piece is the story of a girl at a holiday camp for sight-impaired young people. The youngsters went out in canoes and played games in the woods. One evening I watched Carol Ann, who had no sight, as she found her way round the games room on the outside. I stood back and observed. I admired her skill and confidence. This was not a time to intervene but just to observe. Sometimes we are not needed.

Mapmaker

She walked into the dark sunlight,
the darkness of the unknown,
the unseen,
She was a mapmaker;
sensed the hard patio,
the crunchy gravel,
movable chairs,
pliant grass,
feeling the possibilities,
measuring,
stealing,
usurping,
as she drew
the unseen mind map.
grasped the shape of the day,
north and west,
testing its permanence.

Sun burnt her fair skin.
Wind played with her hair.
She asked questions,
felt the walls,
touched each window,
stroking up and down,
as though befriending
an indulgent horse.

She counted
1, 2, 3 to the corner,
turned through 90 degrees
felt the shape of the room,
three windows,
straight line to the door.
With soft palms and moving fingers
she measured the shiny paint.

Her toes touched a wooden tub.
Hands stretched forward
felt spiny needles,
leaves like wands.
They waved,
greeted her searching fingers,
released faint smell of juniper.
She smiled.

With surveyor's care,
she retraced her path,
to check the reality of the room,
see if 90 degrees still
had the same number,
see if square was still square,
if the world was the same shape,
her map well drawn.

She held the edge
of one open window,
tightened her fingers
on the firm frame.
With her other hand,
she grasped the next,
stood akimbo.

The room was hers;
windows,
door,
tub and tree
were drawn,
counted,
measured,
possessed.

1999
For Carol Ann

We know that the number of people with mental health problems has increased greatly during the pandemic. Before the pandemic, services were struggling and referrals took too long but in 2020 and 2021 the situation has become alarming. Those who have poor mental health are struggling and many, including young people, who have not experienced such problems before, are now finding the isolation, maybe relationship issues, lack of prospects and job losses overwhelming. There is still stigma relating to mental health too, which stops some from admitting to it.

Here is one story of a woman with long term mental health problems. She has found the pressures of three lockdowns have impacted on her health quite severely.

Jen is a woman with bipolar disorder. Her life is up and down in extreme ways. She is bubbly and cheerful, kind and effusive at her best and completely withdrawn for long periods when life is most tough for her. She spends time in the psychiatric unit, where I have visited her. I have also seen her in her home. I wrote this piece after a visit, when she showed me photos of a Caribbean holiday many years previously. I had known her for perhaps 15 years but had not heard before about this holiday. How often we, as chaplains, know people partially, sometimes only aware of the most trying, testing sides of their lives. It was uplifting for us both, I think, to share happy times and beautiful photos.

There or not

You are always there.
The doorbell rings,
door opens, clock ticks,
red blanket comforts the chair,
kettle boils,
air drifts into the room.

You show me a photo,
you both on a beach,
ankles in a far-away sea,
thousands of miles from
this clock-ticking room;
far away from warm red blankets.

So you're not always in this house,
filling the kettle,
bringing out the gold-leafed
visitors' book.
Once you were far away,
warmed by the sun,
toes in the sea,

a different world.

From my Blog 'Three months in Hilpoltstein 2016'

A few years ago, I worked in the Lutheran church in Bavaria for three months. Several times I visited the hospital in the next town. After Brötchen und Kaffee, we met Werner the chaplain. The German for chaplain is Seelsorger, soul carer, a meaningful word. First, he took us to the chapel for 'Andacht', worship. There was only one other man in the chapel. Werner told us that the service is relayed by camera to the wards! What a good idea! Werner spoke in his address of going one step at a time and told the story of a road sweeper who was daunted by the long stretch of road ahead, until he realised that he needed to take one step, one breath and one sweep of the broom at a time. Then it was less daunting. *This resonates with a book by Margaret Silf, 'At Sea with God. She suggests that when it is stormy the 'sailor' could focus on the next sighting of land rather than the end of the journey.*[2]

The chapel has some stunning artwork, wooden doors and panels that show flowing water, rays of sun and a wheat seed. The artist also made a piece showing a couple of people climbing steps and holding out a hand. The leaflet about the artist, Reinhart Fuchs, is inspiring too, in its exploration of the messages in these art works. I found it quite a challenge to read, though inspiring at the same time, rather like poetry. It said that the experience of hospital reminds us in a unique way that we are dependent on strengths outside of ourselves. We are dependent on medical staff, on families and on God's strength. Yet, in this space, we can find our inner strength, can grow and develop.

We, (my husband as a visiting doctor and myself), were privileged to attend a hand-over meeting in the palliative care section of the hospital. Werner, the chaplain, is expected to attend this, which is so different from my experience in England. Nurses and doctors discussed a list of patients, their illnesses, medication, families and whether they might go home. I had a list in front of me which helped me to follow this. Werner took some notes and decided which patients were most in need of a visit.

This level of inclusion is very valuable. One nurse on our children's ward, recently commented on how we, as chaplains, have to go to the patient very sensitively, not knowing whether they've had a tooth removed or have a life limiting condition! It is of course related to issues of confidentiality. As hospital social workers in London in the 70s, we were encouraged to look at the patients' notes and thus we approached them with some knowledge of their situation.

As chaplain in Hereford, I have on one occasion, been part of a multi-disciplinary meeting for end-of-life care. In this area the holistic nature of the needs of the patient are recognized.

This next poem relates to the review of one patient in Roth Hospital, in Germany. There were contributions from nurses, doctors and therapists as well as the chaplain, which indicate a breadth of input and concerns perhaps not apparent in this poem.

Tough sum

She has no smile,
no wardrobe, no menu.

She has such a small story,
loud illness, coded, listed
a sum of what
she has become,
an uncomfortable sum,
that doesn't add up.
it multiplies towards death,

subtracts yesterdays,
sometimes the wings of birds,
the smell of roses,

petals lie scattered,
not counted, jumbled,
in the history of things.

What will be added?
The prayers of a lover,
the smile of the carer,
soft music or faded photo,
colours of Autumn:

Small additions until
the final division.

When being treated for cancer, I wrote the following foot-shaped poem. It expresses a sense of identity as well as uncertainty and hope.

My
Footprints
soft dips in the sheet,
sign of presence, identity
yet going nowhere, uncertain,
waiting for tomorrow's news,
for sunshine, for purpose.
I try them by yesterday's
poem, place them in the
words of hope, step where
monks have been before,
in wilderness and desert.

I hear the tolling bell,
smell the thrift and hope,
catch the drift and gift,
hold the hymn and praise,
pause in the hollow
of pain and love,
print left by Christ.

Section 2

Prayer and spirituality

Prayer is many things. It can be words offered to God, talking, hoping, wondering, expressing thanks or joy. It can be praise or expressing regret or anger. It can be listening. But prayer is much more, as becomes so apparent in the context of the hospital. It can be togetherness, silence, holding hands, lighting a candle, creating a memory box (see later entry).

Prayer

is standing on a bridge
you look
into the deep or dive
into a pool,

you stand
still
in a crowd,
stop
counting,
put away
the tape measure.

you open
your arms, listen
beneath the hum,
sing softly,
chase a

metaphor, you hold
hands, reach for
God's hand

Prayer is stepping
in the dirt, you open
your purse, speak
the truth, share
the picnic
share
stories, take

a hand, carry
a load, walk on
hot sand,
through
undergrowth

you break
bread, wave
a branch, count
bluebells, open
the gates, write
the clouds, wait

for the unknown

It is light slipping in obliquely;
you bathe in its rays,
part the shadows,
smile in the moonlight.

The variety of ways in which the chaplain shares prayer with a patient is diverse and subject to sensitive listening and awareness of his or her needs and spirituality. Words are an important form of two-way communication on the wards, for communicating fears and hopes. But for some patients, there are no words. I met several stroke patients. One stroke survivor wrote 'It is going to be difficult to use words because I know I am losing words… To think that in such a short time and in my own way is coming to me Jesus Christ, that is, I hope, going to look after me, seems a most important thing, but I know it's going to be true, Annie is writing again, Jill is writing, people who know me, love me and will stay with me for ever, all will amaze me.'

On the wards, prayer can be welcomed. I think of GW. From my Placement Journal: 'She had had a stroke, I'd met her before at the chapel service, I wheeled her back to the ward. She was able to convey to me that she's due to go home. Mention of family made her tearful. I'd heard something about her father's murder, so I guessed that may have been part of the cause of her distress. I held her hand and acknowledged her distress, but felt uncertain as to what I should say, not able to engage in conversation. Then I suggested praying together. She agreed, even seemed keen. I prayed for her and her return home, then we said the grace together and *to my delight* she joined in, using the words of the prayer. I have also found the Lord's Prayer and the 23rd Psalm are buried deep in the mind and heart.

If the patient is searching for God or raising Christian issues then prayer, readings and conversation will be relevant, according to the health and situation of the patient. I was asked to visit a woman, Pat, in a coma in a nursing home. In the weeks leading up to this point she had asked her daughters to take her to church. They were surprised, as they were not a churchgoing or believing family. As she had made this request, they sought out a woman priest, (they were quite specific about wanting a woman) and asked me to come. By her bedside, I read the 23rd Psalm, as I imagined that she would have known it as a child. Slowly and reverently, I read it to her in this small room, alongside two anxious daughters. I saw no change in Pat's face or body, but her daughters were sure that their mother reacted to the words of the Psalm and they were both moved and grateful. In this context relationship with distant memories of God, with family and with self, seemed important.

Another occasion I visited an elderly, rather deaf woman in a four bedded ward. I had been asked to see her and knew she wanted prayers, but I faced a dilemma. If I prayed with her about personal issues, the whole ward would hear. If I said a more general prayer, then maybe the other patients could be part of the prayer. *So I settled on the latter.*

There are other times when the background of the patient is unclear and I believe that the patient must take the lead and tell me whatever is on their minds, whatever they are ready to share. If I discover they are Christian, I would then offer a prayer. If this is not the case, I feel that it is not right to offer a prayer, as the patient is vulnerable, lying down, sick and they might well agree just to please the 'well person'. It is widely accepted that the chaplain is not there to persuade the patient of his/her beliefs, but rather to act from the basis of those beliefs, to live out the love of God humbly. The chaplain also needs to be aware of his/her own needs so he/she can hold them back and act just in the patient's interests.

When I was diagnosed with breast cancer, the tables turned, and I was attended to by family, friends and colleagues. They listened to me. I kept a diary and wrote poems, which all helped me to cope. The following is an extract from that diary.

'I dreamt that I was asked to say a prayer on behalf of all of us in the unit for cancer clinics and chemotherapy. Half awake, I took my notebook and wrote the following:

Compassionate, suffering God,
we are here today on a long journey,
uncertain, a little anxious.
Help us to find courage and strength along the way.

May we plan our time, adding in treats,
the pleasures of the garden or countryside,
entertainment, music, meals and visitors
to remind us of life's pleasures and joys.

Help us to love ourselves as we face changes,
to know ourselves as people of value and dignity,
worthy of your love and the love of others.
This can be hard at times, Lord,
as we change in shape and appearance;
but you see beneath the scars;
you see beauty where we fail to.

We are grateful for our friends and family who support us,
for medical staff who treat and guide us.
Help us to be honest and to seek help when we need it.

Maybe we will discover a new set of priorities;
find out what matters most in life
be it friendship, love, relationships or beauty.
help to find value in small things,
to find value in the present moment.
Help us to grow a sense of hope to balance uncertainty,
hope of good things ahead.'

So now I share this prayer with all who read here and hope that it supports and helps all who find themselves in a comparable situation. Rereading this during lockdown, I realise that some of these feelings have emerged during this strange time. Many have spoken of the need for discovering a new set of priorities and finding value in small things.

Having a chapel in a hospital allows for many opportunities for gatherings, for private worship, for a quiet place for relative or patient to pause and reflect, and also for writing in the chapel prayer book. In one hospice chapel I visited, visitors were invited to make a request for prayer or to see the chaplain, by leaving a slip of paper in a box. In another hospital there is an open book where visitors can write their prayers, their gratitude, their anger, their disbelief, or their story. This can be most moving and led to the following two poems.

From a Sad Grandmother

Someone wrote hieroglyphics,
(or was it swear words),
awkward on the page.

Another wrote a list,
asking God for courage,
love, faithfulness.

Next on the page,
was a nameless request,
tidy, careful, full of love.
She asks for reconciliation,
words of grace between Jon and Sarah.

At the bottom of the prayer,
no Elsie or Doris,
simply the words,
'From a Sad Grandmother'

From the pages in the hospital chapel prayer book, July 13

The following poem was inspired by poignant words in the chapel prayer book, which marked the 28th anniversary of a baby's death.

George Felix James

We wrapped you in snowflake patterns,
put you in a box, small as a suitcase.
Closing the lid, we shut out the light,
the sun of our lives, rain of our days.

Where are you my snow baby?

We placed you in the ground; soft, dark place
and planted snowdrops beneath the granite cross,
the hard love cross, fixed and firm,
arms outstretched in the grim winter air.

Those arms reached towards us
and to the desultory visitors,
muffled in the slow wind.
Did those arms hope to touch our frozen hearts?

Where are you George Felix James?

We watch the green beginnings struggle
through the soil, delicate in the cold glimmer
of late winter. We watch the snow-white bells
emerge from their green sheaths.

Baby George, shell of remembrance,
today we light candles for you,
28 snow white candles in the chapel.

We light each year with a sweet sigh,
a small tear,
a mute prayer
for you George Felix James.

Prayers copied from the hospital chapel prayer book. 2005

I hate you!!! How could you do this.

Again God I'm praying to you but why do I feel so alone. I'm pregnant, struggling and all I ask is for my son J to come back home safe. Why is everything in this world so hard Lord?? Just when you feel positive about everything it just goes wrong and you are left feeling desperate. Help me to overcome my feelings of isolation and worry God let me know you are here with us guiding me towards a better life.

To God
Please help me! Can my mum please be pregnant. I am so needing a little brother/sister. I haven't told anyone about this, and I won't.
Thank you for listening God

Riek died at 5.25 tonight. Thank you dearly to all that prayed for him, but it wasn't enough. I never held much of a belief in god and now I know for sure there is no one up there - what a sad, sad thought. My brother was such a lovely sad soul, and we all miss him more than words can express,
his loving sister,
Delci

Thank you, God. Double thanks. Triple thanks.

One Autumn, I heard that a little boy had been born much sooner than expected. I went into SCIBU, Special Care Baby Unit, and there, in the far corner was a tiny baby, fast asleep. I spoke to him quietly and hoped to see his mother. As I knew the family to be Christian, I went away and found Ruth Burgess' 'Book of Blessings' Wild Goose Publishers[3]. One blessing, welcoming the arrival of a new baby, was all about summer, so I rewrote it to reflect the falling leaves and winds of that season. I printed it out, put it in an envelope and propped it at the foot of the small crib. His mother found it later and was delighted with it.

A WELCOME BLESSING for Arthur
Adapted from Ruth Burgess' blessing book

Welcome Arthur.
You arrived with the Autumn colours,
leaves turning red and yellow,
golden and glowing,
shaken by the rainstorms,
warmed by the misty sun.

Welcome Arthur.
May your life unfold
in warmth and beauty.
May the angels protect you
and the saints tell you stories.
May you be caressed and cherished
and cradled in love.

Welcome Arthur.
May you bring joy
to all who meet you.
May you grow each day
in grace and in wonder.
May you be blessed
with the wildness
and wisdom of God.

Chaplains often bring Holy Communion to the patient's bedside, often a pre consecrated, intincted wafer, i.e. one that has been previously blessed at a service of Holy Communion and then dipped into consecrated wine. In my placement journal, I wrote, 'He gave communion to two patients in their beds. I found this moving and meaningful – no candles, no long liturgy, no robes, no stained glass or even Bible, but wafers, a few prayers, drips, tubes, sick bowls, tissues, blanket and three people. It was a stirring mix of the very functional and the holy, signs of sickness and the potentials for being with God in a dark place.'

The following dialogue tells another story of a bedside communion:

Sylvia

Sylvia sits in the small ward, tidy in a pink bedjacket, white hair permed.
Judy knocks and enters, dressed in day clothes with a clerical collar.

Judy: Hello Sylvia
Sylvia : err hello
Judy: I'm Judy, one of the chaplains here, just come to say hallo and see if you want to have a chat.
Sylvia: I've been in here a long time, on another ward - then moved to this one. Seems a long time. *Pause*
I go to St. N's church, or I used to in the old days. It's all changed now, not what it used to be.
Judy: what do you miss most?
Sylvia: I like BCP services and proper hymns, like it was when I was growing up.
She looks into the distance as though seeing her childhood.
I love the old words, ones that we've always said. And I don't hold with women being ordained either. Jesus' disciples were all men, weren't they? *She sighs*
I saw a Catholic priest bringing holy communion to some patients this morning. *She looks around as though seeing the lucky patients.*
Judy: *gently* Well I could bring you communion here in the ward, if you would like?
Sylvia *looks at Judy, the female, ordained chaplain, slightly non-plussed*
Would you? *hope in her eyes*
Yes please, that would be lovely
Fifteen minute later Judy and Sylvia share the intincted wafer, bread of communion, bread of hope, at the bedside.

This child, my granddaughter, was born with hydrocephalus. The early weeks and months were very worrying. This birth clearly made an impact on me that was very personal. In Kathryn Mannix' book 'With the End in Mind' [4] she relates the experience of her being at the side of her grandmother, as she faced death. There she learnt in a personal way, a little more of what grief means, and the part that the family plays. Our personal experience adds to our arsenal of understanding.

But in this instance, Naomi grew to be a happy, healthy child.
Here I am thinking of Naomi from far away. Prayer can sometimes be uttered from afar and consoles the prayer as much as the recipient.

A Candle for Naomi

I light a candle for you Naomi,
a small yellow glow
in the corner of a chapel,
by the edge of a lake,
beneath the mountains,
under the mist,
near the edge of Wales

I light a candle for you Naomi
and will leave it there to burn,
there to pray, there to glow,
as I drive away,
leaving this valley behind,

as you lie in your cot,
in St. Anne's hospital,
in the busy city,
near the port,
as you feed and watch,
as you wave and wriggle,
this candle burns for you.

October 2012

I spent my sabbatical partly on the Lleyn Peninsula, in West Wales, visiting the church, the island and the wild coast, where R. S. Thomas lived and ministered for the last years of his life. We listened to talks by a professor and we met his son. The depths of this poet's words, the intrigue of his thinking came alive to us. I enjoyed his poetry, the ambiguity, the sense of questioning and mystery. I enjoyed the way he likened prayer to the waves coming and going. There is something mysterious about prayer which is apt when we look at the God to whom we pray. It is fitting to think of such prayer in the context of the hospital ward, like a rhythm in the background, an ongoing pulse that fuels the love and the listening.

Prayer Beach *in response to Tidal by R.S.Thomas*

Waves crumple up the beach.
They break and retreat;
again and again, like prayer,
hope, longing and questioning;
They curl into the bay towards the
old tractor, the small black dog,
and the boys fishing.

R.S. writes of the God of fissures,
craggy spaces where prayer may rest.
Prayers flow towards them,
bend in obeisance,
turn and try again,
The sand murmurs,
whispers in response.

The bay embraces the attempt;
its arms hold me still as time stops.
The rocks gleam and say the time
in their black faces.
Time here is a salty prayer,
waves pound my heart;
slices and crags fill with water.
Is God here?

Is it the poem I'm admiring
or the shock of the meaning?

Prayer may be enigmatic or mysterious, but that leads to the question; what do we mean by spirituality? The World Health Organization recognises spirituality as a core dimension to improve quality of life for the patient and the family. John MacQuarrie writes, 'Spirituality is not a retreat or escape into an inner world, for spirit is precisely the capacity to go out, and the truly spiritual person is the one who is able to go out or to exist in the full dynamic sense' There are many different traditions of Christian spirituality. Many live in the 'alternation of prayer and action. Prayer as we have seen is the concentration of explicit moments of that which is supportive of all life, while action is in turn suffused with prayer'. He refers to 'an ever-deepening vision and communion for we have seen that the Christian pilgrimage does not come to an end but always keeps its dynamic character. [5]

From this I would particularly draw the notion of dynamic fusion of prayer and action. Richard Rohr wrote 'We come to God through things as they are; spirituality is about sinking back into the Source of everything. We're already there, but we have too little practice seeing ourselves there.' [6] Through these words we see the possibility of a profound relationship with God and all that there is.

The first and last poems in this section which explore prayer has some Christian imagery, but it might also relate to other faiths. In the hospital, chaplains often meet with people of other faiths or none. Often there will be chaplains available for those of other faiths, sometimes not. Often the chaplain will visit a patient who has no commitment to any religious body. But still each person has a spiritual side to them. What might this mean?

In the following resumés of explorations of spirituality in the wider sense, relationship is frequently cited, relationship which is dynamic. Pulaski refers to relationship with self, with nature, connectedness to the moment and to the sacred or 'other'.

In the Buddhist exploration of the meaning of spirituality we find 'searching for meaning' which is an active dynamic process and could embrace many of the other definitions. For me, this search is carried out through the medium of words, exploring ways of expressing difficult or complex ideas, or expressing the inexpressible. Poetry lends itself to this search, whether writing or reading it. In the Buddhist approach, 'peace of mind' is cited which could be one result of the search. Peace is a state of being which is particularly desirable at the end of life. Kathryn Mannix writes of using Cognitive Behavioural Therapy to explore the mental processes of a patient to help him understand why he is panicking and how to channel it.

All these ideas of spirituality touch on relationship, to self, to nature, to others, sometimes including a higher being, connectedness and a search for meaning too. The role of the chaplain includes listening out for these issues, listening to what is said and even what is not said and supporting the patient in his or her journey. On some occasions it means providing tools, such as prayer, holding a hand, (when this is wise in relation to infection) or supporting with a difficult encounter or conversation.

Section 3

On the edge

Disability

Moltmann: Maybe we need to turn to those who have deep experience of powerlessness to find out how to live!! [7]

Pooh: Sometimes it's a boat and sometimes it's an accident. It all depends on whether I'm on top of it or underneath it.'

I invite you on a visit with me - come with me to the day centre - it's called 'Headway'.

A woman called Sheila is talking to her neighbour; we can hear her saying how hard it is to answer the phone as she couldn't find the right words. - she can't remember numbers or write anything down as she's lost the use of her right arm. More people arrive. Pete leaning heavily on a stick and Jim in a wheelchair—they, like most of the people here, have lost their jobs, their income — Ted sitting there he's in a wheelchair too —his marriage has fallen apart—Mark's personality changed so he was subject to anger that was hard to control. They'll go and play dominos soon I expect.

Another woman (I'll call her Joan) leads me outside and asks me to light her cigarette for her—as a non -smoker I find this a very strange thing to be doing – but strangely intimate and moving!!
There's a specially laid out garden with raised beds. I haven't been here in the summer, but I'm told many centre users get satisfaction from planting and tending plants out here.
I've just seen the music therapist arrive—she has a room set apart where centre users are invited or encouraged to go and express themselves—sounds very valuable.

The church has given much serious thought to the place of disabled people in our society. I read an article written by Rev Richard Green who was Disability Minister for our deanery. The main thing that stood out for me, was the importance of stressing the disabled person's ability not disability! I am reminded of Penny who made a pot as a present for her mother —and Mark who made everyone laugh with his jokes. Someone else wrote stories—these things were so important. Many of the activities at the centre allowed them to be realistic about the damage they had suffered but also offered them ways of finding new things they could do.

Jesus was very real about people—he accepted them just as they were— the woman with the haemorrhage would have been a social outcast in those days (as would those who were disabled, as we call it today. How much have we changed in that regard?) —but Jesus was ready to help her—he accepted people as they were, as well as seeing their potential for change —he shocked the very religious by eating with the sinners and refusing to condemn the adulterer. He could see what they could become. and also encouraged the crowd to accept that they were not perfect either.

It can be in weakness and trauma that we actually find a new sense of direction—it is a place where God works through us, uses us to be his own.

Magnificat

God is a space

holding suffering -

a space which may have walls,
may have a floor, where footsteps meet.

God is a space, sometimes without a name -
strong enough for blunt words,
gracious enough for sadness.

God is the space where I sit,
seeing the man's anger,
deadened by despair,

surrounded by white walls,
coloured curtains,
shared cup,
broken bread.

God is the bread allowed to break,
crumbs fall like tears,
the breaking is the start of something new.

This one imagines the sense of loss, the grief felt by those who suffer brain damage, and their families feel this too.

Song of Loss
(Headway)

I look into his face,
deep into the eyes,
the dull, staring, hopeless eyes,
see the shock.
He finds himself
a shadow person,
a ghostly image,
mockery of his true self.

I play 'My First Loss' on the keys,
slow stretching, eternal notes,
arching, empty, and sad,
moving over the abyss,
the white notes
in aching tune.

I know the ache of losing a friend,
like losing a part of yourself.
I have lost parts of myself at times,
hopes and expectations have fallen away,
but never half a body,
parts of a life,
words, history.
I have lost days, energy and numbers.
Yes, I have known loss,
but not walking, talking, thinking,
parts of the brain and its order.

As I listen to the confusion
hear the song of the dispossessed,
I join in the plaintive harmonies.

We need to find new parts of ourselves,
new appointments, new love,
new pots, new patterns,
new tunes and new jokes.

2002

This again talks of God's ability to hold suffering but then moves on to re-count the blessings that God can lend to the sufferer. God lets us share his creativity and through our diverse creations lets us grow and find peace.

God in a manger

God is big enough to hold suffering,
gracious enough to embrace sadness,
life anger, labour pain, love ache.
God holds them like a womb;
God gives pages for poems,
staves for songs,
a stable for new hope.

God is close enough to share our joy,
our celebrations, our feasts,
God lends rhyme to our poetry,
harmony to our song;
shows us glimpses
of light and love,

The following poem arose from an account of a man with dementia. He used the phrase 'forgive my forgets'. I found this phrase apt, and it pointed to a story. Hence the ensuing rendering in a poem.

Forgive my forgets

'Forgive my forgets'
Small blue flowers,
clustered, brief flowers,
pale grace, gifts of the
season, grown in the
corner of childhood,

Forget me nots, easily
missed, as on a misty
day, words, thoughts
slip between the hours,
confound you Simon,
until the light shines

and you remember
'Forgive my forgets'.
'Forget me not,'
'forgive those lost
words, those vanishing
names. Let them go.'

‘Forgive my forgets
Don’t forget me'. Re-
member those small
blue flowers, hiding
in your memory, shy
in your childhood,

Calling your names,
remembering your
forgets, on the edge
of words, the frail rim
of conversation, 'for-
give me my forgets.'

'Forgive me my flowers,
my long-lost blossoms,
forgive me my blue, my
green. Scatter them in
my dreams, as they fall
helplessly through my

fingers. Their scent melts
into the past.
Forgive
me

my

forgets.'

I visited a nursing home during the pandemic. Visiting was restricted. The husband in this poem had to stand outside the building, talking to his demented wife through a small crack in the window. His next move impressed me.

Rainbow words

He is poised by the window,
a slight stir of outside air
waves into the wife's room.

She stares, face bemused,
thatch of pure white word
looks blue into his masked face

His book of sonnets speaks
familiar buzz words, extraordinary
love words through the permitted crack.

She mutters green words, mixed-
up orange words, rainbow words

in the patient, white-arranged room.

All is puzzled white, crazy red,
tangled green and orange,
except for the pure stream

of rhyme and rhythm, quatrains
and couplets, rise and music
from the ancient bard.

It is nearly Christmas, red and
green season, golden glimmer
season, love and song season.

Let's all celebrate with the wordless,
with the rainbow people, the
tangled and tortured folk

Alleluia

I met George in the local Tesco's. I stopped and we chatted about his life which I tell here.

George

George sits on a wooden chair.
The dog half sleeps at his feet.
People pass with trolleys,
eyes fixed on supper;
eyes green, brown, rainbow,
crystallised on some dream.

George's eyes are round,
blue as space,
hard as stone,

opaque as cloud.
Lola looks keenly,
licks with greeting
and the story starts.

The Belfast accent opens the
page,
intro over, narrative flows,
Ballyhack, Newtownards,
blind centre moved away,
marriage over, life dissolving.
George sits on a wooden chair,
holds a talking sat nav,
a long way from Belfast.

Emma was a pupil at a special school. Her mental age was about 18 months whereas her real age was 17. A speaker came to the school and talked about age-appropriate teaching. She gave examples, relating to explaining menstruation to girls with limited understanding. Explaining the biology and relationships to more able girls (and boys), then several stages of lesser complexity for less able girls. At Emma's level she suggested reassurance that blood loss once a month was normal, was needed, if indeed she was aware of her periods at all. Reassurance would need to be with smiles and facial acceptance as she understood no words.

Emma

She sits in the sunlight,
grey eyes move
like floating flecks of dust.
Someone holds her hand,
admires the colour of her dress.

How do our words seem to her?
like the flow of water over her hands
or the sunlight on her face?

She faces a boy,
who sits askew on a trike,
but her eyes don't change,
as he pushes with his feet and topples.

What do the colours,
the wheels, or the legs mean to her?
What does Jack's cry do to her?
Does it flicker in her young breast?

Emma has learnt to smile
when her name is called.
she knows her name,
those four letters,
that warm, shell-like name,
that round sound.

But the roundness of her womb
will stay a mystery,
the journey of the egg,
rhythms over the years,
music which ebbs and flows,
hopes and failings.

The blood flow will,
leave her like a sigh.
She'll feel warm hands and words
like a cocoon around her
and not know that blood is red.

Daniel (a very troubled child)

A small boy calmed his tears and shouts,
noticed the world around him,
smiled at the Christmas feast,
leant towards me and said:
'Here you are.
Take this and spend it on yourself!'
Into my hand he pressed a 5 pence coin!
A small boy whose life shuddered like an earthquake,
now spoke like a kind uncle –
used grown up words,
startling, from this 8-year-old body,
poised from a shaken life-point.

I met Martha crossing the road with her shopping. Her slow gait and preoccupation with walking drew my attention.

Martha Jones

The light's red.
She crosses slowly,
stooped like a head of barley,
care-full hands on her trolley,
her shopping, tea, jam,
sausages and greens,
stored in the deep, black bag.

Foot after foot,
teeth gritted in pain,
she looks towards home,
beyond the walking light.
She looks into emptiness,
into the space, where
tomorrow should be.

Fingers tense with the task,
shoulders hunched with the weight
of it all, ham, beans and pork pie.
Step by step, she gets there,
no eyes to left or right,
no nod or wave to Tim,
Jack or Harry who wait in their cars.

They do not exist;
there's nothing but baked beans,
heavy potatoes and custard;
nothing but the steamy plod
across the pausing space,
the black summer journey,
her Sunday jaunt.

She reaches the pavement,
turns right and onwards,
homeward she plods
her weary day,
pushing the butter, fish and tea bags,
like a whale gathering plankton,
knowing nothing but the swim and the plod,
the job and the catch.
The lights are green for
Tim, Jack and Harry.
They drive away,
leave Martha Jones
to plod and patter
along the flagstones,
towards the harbour of home

I noticed this unkempt man on the station platform. He finds his way into this book, as a person on the edge of society, someone who is left out. May-be he has no home or family, but that is pure speculation. I met characters not unlike him when in hospital. He reminds me of the small elf like man I met once in a ward who entertained us by playing the spoons.

The Blue Case

My case is a new chance.
Inside, socks, pyjamas, soap.
I become an inch taller,
straighten my woolly hat;
I almost smile. I tenderly
pull the zip. It slides along
the blue case. I look again
at my new life, as rain falls
on the platform.

The announcer talks of
cancellations, floods.
My eyes stare in the cold air.
People nudge and jostle.
I look at the case again!
the silver stripe, handle,
wheels fit for heaven.
Where will it take me?

The Baptist Church runs clubs for people in the city. On a Friday, a group of homeless people gather for a good lunch and various activities. I was invited to take a series of Creative Writing Workshops. It proved exciting, engaging, funny and sad. I have no records of their work except for a thank you card. One man wrote 'your wisdom is a big luv'. It is a profound statement. It is also striking that it comes from a man in tough circumstances and little education.

Several homeless people come into the hospital chapel. I remember one woman whom I knew, coming in with a few street friends. She was Sharon and I had met her on the bus with her children and mother. We had spoken and I had learnt the children's names. Somehow it had all gone wrong, and Sharon ended up living on the streets. But by the time I met her this time, she had a flat to live in and social workers were helping her to put her life together again.
Sharon and her friends arrived at the door of the chapel seeking consolation. They were upset at the death of a friend, the fourth in as many months. They came to remember him. They were keen to speak of the lives of these fellow street dwellers.

Section 4
Exile

These poems bring us to new places, places that are unfamiliar, where we need to adjust. Some bring us to situations of conflict where many of us have never been. Maybe there is something that resonates however, something that strikes a chord, reminds us of being apart in a strange place. Here, many emotions are at play, and I suspect that those who have suffered life-changing or chronic illness will have experienced something like these.

The first one is a reflection on lockdown during 2020. During this time, we have found ourselves in a new place, facing isolation, fear or apprehension. In this poem I describe a sense of something new, or some new sensitivity within me. I am aware of new depths, new searching, new responses arising from this unique situation. I search for wisdom, mentioning the psalms. I find new rhythms and value in silence. Yet still aware of the needs of others, the neighbour who longs for communion.

Below the water lily

I find my rhythm, the slow beat
of minims. I hear the music
of a hundred years, half hidden
promises of unexpected cadences.

I find my soul, waiting patiently
to say its name. I ask it questions.
Hold its murmured answers.
I live the silence, find there
new sighs and vibrations.

I open a poem, let it walk through my veins.
I read a psalm, touch the fringes
of its ancient wisdom. I look beneath
the beauty of the water lily.

I dive below the upbeat of my heart,
measure the meaning of new syllables.
I write in the mystery depths
of lost spaces, sense a new presence.

I listen between the words
of a neighbour's tale. From
afar, I hold her anxious hand,
promise bread and wine - next year.

This poem was written while I was being treated for cancer. There lies here a sense of questioning, a sense of wondering and marking change. When we are sick, we often ask many questions, feel a sense of bewilderment and uncertainty. This short poem ends with a determination to make progress.

Thistledown

Where am I? That is the question.
Yesterday I had feet
Yesterday I played the trumpet
Yesterday I baked bread

Now the smell lingers
the sound echoes
footsteps fade

Where am I? That is the question

I fall as bare snowflakes
I dance as thistledown
I blur as a soaked script
I sigh as a silent full stop
I whisper as wind in the grass

Where am I? I ask

Tomorrow I will sound the horn
Tomorrow I will shout the news
Tomorrow I'll walk through the rainbow
and spread a feast on the new table.

The poem 'Label' highlights loss of identity in a small child in the Congo. The child has no name or identifying features. It is full of pathos and pain. Patients in a hospital often feel lost, their usual routine is gone, their usual sense of self is shaken, their future may well be unknown.

The label hangs before the poem
(Congo child)

It's hard to write the story of a nameless child,
with no words,
no smile, no touch, no scream,
no picture, or chart, but just a label,
pink and orange clothes and a label.

Solemn brown feet, no dance,
or kick, no stamp or speed,
no greeting or game,
no glint or grin,
just a label,
with size, brand and wash code;

no age, no name, no song
no blink, no plea, no murmur,
just pink shorts with a label;
no voice, no preference, no mattress,
no trail, no home, no address,
just pink shorts with a label.

2009

The next poem is a response to an extreme situation. The sculpture is of a man with a suitcase, but only one arm and no body. He has left part of himself behind in his homeland. It gives the viewer a sense of near horror. What must it be like to have to leave your home, maybe family and job and travel in difficult, challenging circumstances to a new place and start your life again from scratch? I suggest that some of the same emotions and experiences may arise when a man or woman has a severe illness, perhaps a stroke. They have huge adaptations to make. They may have lost speech and mobility. They may have to stop working, stop playing football or driving a car. It may feel as though they have left some of their body and mind behind. They may well have to start again. They will need courage and resilience, hope and humour, as well as support from staff and family.

The trudge of Exile

After a sculpture by Joe Locke

I walk, half of me
black against the sky;
gnawed by the rats of heart ache,
eaten by the trudge of exile.

The light sees me in part;
my body casts little shadow;
my case is my prop. It holds
me in the unknown air.

My legs know no master,
my head no breath,
my single arm no blood.
I freeze against the alien landscape,
hard as metal, cold as dry bones.

I am the statue of exile.

This poem retells one small, but striking story of the struggles of wartime. The theme of bread is poignant to a Christian. Bread is a symbol of Jesus, his life, our communion with him, our hope. The third verse echoes something of the story of the 'feeding of five thousand.' Bread is significant to the Jewish tradition too, with the unleavened bread taken while the Israelites were fleeing from slavery in Egypt – a symbol of flight and rescue. A patient too will often search for meaning and the essentials of life.
The poem ends holding on to hope.

Loaves and Wishes

Outside the bakery
bread vans are pocked with holes.
Two drivers are dead.

The last vat is only half full
of soft, living but dwindling dough,
symbol of hope and determination.
Its poignant smell mixes with smoke,
with the stench of war and misery.

Today there will be five hundred loaves,
to share among thousands.
Tomorrow—
no fuel, no water,
the huge mixer blades will stand still;
yet another fatality of the burning strife.

Hope must not die with these last loaves!

Sarajevo Oct '92

Here we enter into a world most of us know little about. This girl and some of the characters we meet alongside her, have been thrown out of their normal world. They are living in a new space and feel a range of emotions, bewilderment, isolation and fear or maybe determination and resilience. They are exiles in some way. This sense of being torn away from the familiar and comfortable is known to some who are suddenly taken ill, who are rushed to hospital and whose life suddenly changes direction. They will probably experience some of these emotions. this selection of poems from around the world suggest that these emotions are shared across continents and during different world changing events. Some people have expressed some of these feelings during the recent pandemic in enforced isolation.

This girl has no name, and I can only imagine what she was feeling. I only meet her in a photo in a newspaper. So, I must admit to entering imaginatively and yet tentatively into her situation. I draw on the personal armoury of emotions that I have built up in my life, including illness and loss, as well as listening to others, professionally and personally. I see her as representative of her people in a time of conflict. I can do no more. Sadly, this poem still resonates in 2022 as the people of Afghanistan again suffer under the Taliban regime.

The Afghan Girl

I look at her,
beautiful girl,
face busy,
dress coloured.

I note the angle of her turning,
the way she holds him,
her young brother,
as though he were her own child.

She's framed among words,
still, for all to see,
an icon of these days.

She is Afghanistan.
She is her people.
She is the crowd of refugees,

the flying people,

Again, a story about being in a foreign place, not knowing what the future holds, about fear and the strength of family ties. It is also a story of hearing loss. The loss of any sense can impede communication, which is so central to our living. These emotions may resonate with some patients who face new challenges and uncertainties.

Tell us your story Yousef.

I feel lost and scared. We've come a long way, left our home in ruins. That shook us all, my Mum, my Dad, my sister and me, the noise was horrid. I put my hands over my ears, not that I can hear as well as you. The house shook, walls crumbled, and people screamed. That was the worst bit, a high screeching sound that even I could hear. Then the shaking and vibrations everywhere. My Dad grabbed my hand and we tumbled into the street. I looked round for Maryam. I don't like to go far from her, but Dad tugged my arm, so it hurt. We coughed and choked as the street filled with smoke and dust. Where is my mum and Maryam? I wanted to shout but the dust stopped my words.

By the end of the day, we were miles away; we found Mum and Maryam and we cried and coughed, laughed and shouted; it was so good to be together. We walked and walked. Our feet hurt; my shoes were a bit small anyway and now my toes felt squashed and sore.

We walked on and on with lots of other people; some were neighbours, others complete strangers, but it helped to be together. They began to sing; I suppose it cheered them up. My hearing aids weren't working very well, and it sounded far away. I didn't sing. We slept that night under a tree. It got cold when dark set in. I held onto Maryam, and we tried to keep each other warm. That was days ago, don't know how many. We crossed into Turkey, and I could feel Dad grip my hand less hard. I think he was relieved to get over that border.

Now we're in Istanbul, a huge, busy place. My hearing aids are not much good now. I can feel the rumble of traffic; it travels through my bones. When they want to talk to me, they turn my face to theirs. It feels warm and hopeful, their hands pressed against my cheeks. Their lips move, open and close and I have to guess what they're saying. If it's about food, I'm better at guessing; the smell helps and the sight of red cherries or steaming potatoes certainly make sense.

I hope I can get new hearing aids. I can't hear much at all. I don't know where we're going, what will happen to us? Can we stay here? Or will we walk again? I want to know what will happen.
One day we're in some building, a Christian church, I think. A woman talks to me, though I don't know what she's saying. She then talks to my parents. I think they're planning something. After this we go to a place where they mend hearing aids. Can they help me?

Now suddenly, my world has changed, voices, music, traffic all sound just as they used to. My mum says thank you to the woman and we walk along a busy shopping street. Horns blare, a street musician plays his guitar, a train roars in the distance. I walk with Mum and Dad just behind Maryam. They are laughing and I wonder if they're going to sing?

Can you feel the sound of the tractor?

For Evelyn Glennie

Can you feel the sound of the tractor,
its rumble in your belly? Shudder in your bones?

Can you sense the tremble of the birdsong,
the call that colours the air?

Can you sense the laughter of the ducks,
as they flap through spring air?

Can you discern the swell of the choir,
as they welcome the dawn of Easter?

Can you feel the buzz of bees,
as their nest is disturbed?

Can you grasp the lapping of the water,
as it caresses the shores of the lake?

Can you sense the music of the stream,
as it tumbles over rocks to our delight?

Can you feel the sound of the tractor
as it tows the straw to storage?

I know you can, because you told me so,
but I struggle to write it down
as I only listen;

I ignore the buzz
and the rumble, the tremble, shudder,
and the beating of the air.
I just listen.

In the summer of 2010, miners were trapped underground in Chile for many months, as plans were devised to bore a hole deep down and rescue them. Someone let down miniature Bibles with Psalm 40 marked and lenses to make them readable.

Sometimes a Bible verse will help people to find a way through a difficult time. These miners found the words of David helpful, and they could make use of his story and hope. They were clearly trapped and needed a vision of rescue.

In a similar way, oppressed peoples in South America have used the Exodus story to inspire them. They turn to the God of liberation and tune their journey with the Israelites' trudge through the wilderness. It gives them hope of change and rescue (as Bishop Peter Selby called salvation)[8]

Life at the end of a rope

David on his death bed
unearthed sounds of praise:
he honoured the power of limitation,
the focus offered by life's transience.

A poem sings through its regulation:
music soars, formed by tonality,
so the knowledge of death gives power to life.

Hope let down by a rope
into the dark of the mine trap,
hope in a psalm, magnified with lens,
bursts open the possibilities of that 20-day prison,

magnified by the dank threat of death,
lit by the crevice-squeezed shaft of overhead noon;
the plea, expressed in miniature,

touches them in the stricture of the space,
the confines of the rock face,
the concentration of days.

David-words of miry pit
and mud and clay give way
to escape and freedom,
light and air, friend and beer.

2010

Section 5
End of life

In this section we find a series of brief stories of patients and others who are at the end of their lives. I have been reading Dr Kathryn Mannix' book called 'With the End in Mind'. (previously mentioned) She writes this book for everyone, for we will all experience death at some point, our own or before that, the death of someone close to us. Her goal is to try and take away the fear that some people have of witnessing the process of dying or of facing death themselves. She gently asks people what they expect and tells them what is most common in the days leading up to death. She gently details changes in breathing and an increase in sleep and she emphasises that it is often a peaceful, fearless time.

Cicely Saunders' biography tells us the important story of the birth of the hospice movement.[9] This amazing woman stressed the value of the last weeks or days of a person's life. It matters how a person lives at this time and how staff assist, treat pain, encourage quality of life. She described the former attitudes of many doctors whose motivation in practising medicine was to cure people, give them more life and turn their sickness around. But Cicely Saunders, who was a nurse, a social worker and finally a doctor with a strong Christian faith came to see things differently and challenge this prevailing attitude.

Here we meet a number of people coming to the end of their lives. We share their stories and empathise with their actions and feelings. We start with a young man, keen to wrap up Christmas presents early for his family, in case he doesn't live long enough to give them to his parents, twin brother and older brothers.

Five Gifts

He wrapped gifts for his mum
and his dad, for his three brothers,
carefully tucking in the ends,
sticking up the corners,
writing names on each one.

It was weeks before Christmas,
fairy lights were switched on,
evenings were dark and cold.
Shoppers were clicking on line

or visiting the shopping malls.

Yes, it was beginning, the
Christmas hope, the run up
to panic, the surge to excess.
But he beat them to it; put
the scissors away, the tape

in the drawer, the four gifts
on the chest by the door,
ready in case; 'In case I'm not
here' he said. 'I want you
to have something from me'.

The family gulped back tears
and waited. What else could
they do? Then on Christmas
day, he gave them the five
precious gifts, his last.

There has been an outpouring of story and poetry since Mark's death. His story as he left it was published, as well as a book of poems documenting his final years written by his mother, poet Susan Jane Sims[10]

Here we read about an older man, reaching the end of his life, facing some confusion:

Patterned by Peacocks

You lie there,
patterned by life,
roving eyes searching for truth.
You see a rose and two cyclists;

you question the pictures on the wall
and you wonder when it'll be time for church.

You lie there,
patterned by hospital.
You watch nurses with bed pans,
patients with Zimmer frames.
You catch floating words
and imagined tunes.

You've always loved tunes,
grand tunes and great narratives.
Now they rumble around in competition;
a relay, or a three-legged race,
a sack race, with truth bundled into pockets;
an obstacle race, with rails and lifts,
with trays and trumpets.

Now your ninety-five your old stomach hurts.
That last jump was too high.
You lie at the finishing line,
the race nearly done.

You lie there,
patterned by peacock and butterflies.
You've folded up your sack,
put away your running shoes.
You no longer jump
or sigh.
In the summer light,
you seek where God has been.

Encounters at the end of life can be charged with emotion. They can be an opportunity for honesty and love, a time for prayer and friendship. The depth of this next poem explores this.

Visiting with Miriam

Life before us
life behind us
life around us

Love between us
love over us
love beneath us

Tears between us
tears welling in us
tears falling from us

Emptiness haunting us
emptiness crying in us
emptiness holding out her hand

Pain painted by us
depths visited by us
pleading voiced in us

Prayer between us
prayer arising in us
prayer holding us in her arms

God watching us
God hurting with us
God loving in us

The following poem depicts a death like those Kathryn Mannix describes, peaceful, gradual and warm. This does not deny the huge grief and sense of loss felt by the family. Helen was only 38 and had a young family. She was encouraged to write a letter to her children for them to read at some later time. I was asked to read the following poem at Helen's funeral. The family asked that the cremation service should not mention God. My colleague honoured that request, of course, but said to me, that in her mind, whenever she mentioned the word ‘love’ for her it meant God.

Helen

The candle burns still,
intense glow,
alive,
the hour’s heat,
slow, calm,
giving.

vibrant,
generous evening,
sunset orange,
last rites.

Friends sit round,
cupping the warmth.

Flame flickers,

yellow gutters,

smoke wafts
into the starless night.

Warm wax

drips

slowly

down

the slender body.

In sudden,
black chaos,
all shiver.

In their eyes.
light quivers still.

Another calm, dignified death, where relationship to self, others and God are good. This time the patient was elderly and ready to go.

The Sun goes down

As the golden light creeps
between green foliage,
as the day ticks quietly by,
I see where she lies.
I see her in her garden room,
sun shining among the trees,
sinking, as it does, before
our sun in the west.

Her sun is going down,
an orange glow, a ball
of fire and warmth, a slow,
but dignified retreat from
the world of trees, flowers,
nurses and children.

The sun will rise again
and again, but Janet's
surprises have surely
come to an end.

It can be hard when a loved person is dying and they are many uncrossable miles away. Writing and poetry can ease the sadness and lessen the gap. Others will find music or even being alongside water will ease the strain.

Walking along the shore

(remembering Helen Patey, music therapist)

I walk on the crunchy shore,
black stones shift beneath my feet.
You are not walking now.

I walk along the wavy shore,
waves come and go,
time comes and goes;
shores mark a beginning or an ending.
You are at a shore,
where days end and expanse waits.
'At the end, there is a beginning'.

I pick up fossils, to name or date;
they are older than you or me,
older than hands or feet;
they have seen people come and people go.

The wind chases the water,
tousles my hair,
the air fresh and disturbing.
Your wind struggles, comes and goes,
precious new wind enters your lungs.

Birds call, loud, raucous, informative.
Your music called, sensitive and probing,
opening cradle minds and closed days.
You gave the gift of calling to many,
calls which will not go away.

A TB clinic stands grey on the hill;
patients used to lie outside in fresh air beds;
you lie in your hospice bed,
sharing times with your daughter.

The sun glows gold, throwing its colour
across the western sky,

This poem emphasises the waiting nature of the end of life. Once again putting words on paper can fill the aching time.

Paper Trail

This delicious paper, white as ice cream,
blank as a full moon,
this generous paper, wide as an ocean,

waiting like a penitent, ready as a bride.
I am in a waiting room, waiting for my scan,
a picture that will tell a story. I sit by an open door.

Norman is waiting too, lying on a white sheet.
The door stays open, as he shares his waiting.
The sun rises and blesses the roses; then it sets.

Norman opens his eyes and smiles.
He sleeps and dreams.
It is a waiting game, we say, though no fun.

We wait from dawn to dusk, texting, talking, listening.
We smell the roses and stare at the moon.
The clock ticks, as the hands move slowly round.

This generous paper, white as a bed sheet,
fills with waiting words, invites more and more.
It is hospitable to ice cream and roses.

At the end of life, there can be special moments of closeness. Kathryn Mannix describes a family with a dying father, two distraught daughters and a calm wise stepmother. During the last few hours, the daughters and stepmother's conversations cover important ground, saying to each other how important they are to one another and have been to the dying father and partner.

In this poem the sharing of special words and wisdom create an unforgettable bond. Michael Mayne describes three different levels of human conversation from the superficial through to 'the confession that we are fellow men, full of fear and anguish, calling for help.' He says that it is in this 'sharing of affliction and helplessness, that the fruit of love can grow'. [11]

This poem remembers an honest conversation towards the end of life. it was the final year of Terry Waite's time as a hostage. He was to be released later that year and somehow his situation reverberated with the days before this death.

My Mother and Me, with hostage and monk.

Time befriended us.
She stood still,
embraced our sharing.
All our yesterdays
crowded into the room,
our journeys, our stories,
our speaking, our silences.

There, on that settee,
there, in that flowery, familiar room,
that space of story and symphony,
in that stillness, we shared words,
words that tussled with life,
cradled death in its timelessness.
We were in synchrony,

like notes in a chord,
like hands on the clock.
We trod the pages
of history, entered the cell
of the hostage, the prayer
of the monk, and gracious
time let us in,
into her Kairos moment.

That hour is now framed
in memory, now hangs
in the gallery of time,
lodged in the booklet of death,
prized in the chronicle of life,
serving as the stepping-
stone of all our tomorrows.

This is a story of Tim who had had a stroke, told by his wife. It is warm and there is a sense of humour here, which helps this family to manage daily struggles.

Five Words

He watches and listens, says little.
'Speak!' she urges 'Say something to me.
Can you give me a sentence?'

He looks at her and slowly
with a glint in his eye, says,
'Will you kiss me?

'one, two, three, four,' she counts,
asking for one more word.
He looks her in the eye and says,

'Will you kiss me now?'
Five words and a request
she cannot refuse!

A story of a small boy with a life limiting illness.

Toby is 4

A loved child, thin and wasted,
held a woolly lamb in his arms,
a cream toy, soft and symbolic.
He held the Christ image in his hands
and walked unsteadily towards the crib.
He laid it gently by the wooden manger
at the feet of a pink, plastic Jesus.
Tears blurred his mother's eyes.
He turned, staring blankly at no one
and sat down by the other children.

In Muheza hospital, Tanzania, as an ordinand, I was invited to join morning worship with the nurses. Later that week I attended a clinic for palliative care. It was a new notion then, in Africa in 2002, the idea that the care of those near to death was a valuable, important medical and social endeavour. A special building, to be named the Diana Centre, was underway. But, at that time, the doctor, Karilyn Collins, used a room in the main hospital. I was asked to take coffees and teas to the patients. I learnt the Swahili words for these drinks but was very aware of the limits of my communications. I couldn't hear the stories of these people, only bring them a drink and share smiles. They benefitted from time together with other patients, time to share with others, rather than stand in a long line in the hot sun waiting to be seen, inevitably fairly briefly, before returning some distance, quite likely on foot, to their homes.

Years earlier, further west in Tanzania, we visited another hospital, and I recorded this visit in my diary. Recently it became a poem.

Candles at the Plantation Hospital

A candle waited and a match.
'Please' said a nurse,
so I took a match, struck it,
held still the flame,
aware of patients
behind the door.

Gently, I lit the candle,
solemn, sensing honour.
The door opened in welcome.
.........'Karibu'......
Two pregnant women,
wrapped in bright cloths,
known as 'kitenges'; babies,
children in cots, some sharing.

At the next ward,
another candle,
a few sick, old men,
some with malaria.
Dull eyes returned our gaze.

If only they might sense
the light, smile, song
in the African sun.

Outside in brightness,
we gathered to fine song,
chants, swaying, red,
blue, orange kitenges.
A trolley, wooden,
with small wheels was
pushed into the yard.
There, a whole goat,
roasted with head, ears,
hooves and tail.

As lighter of candles,
I sat on the high table,
with knife and fork to
cut my portion of goat,
and a bottle of coke.

In the yard, flamed
a brilliant red Christmas tree:
gifts handed to nurses
to cheers and ululation.
Thanks and sunlight
now cheered the day.

I wonder if the women
and the old men in the wards
could hear the jubilation.

A short acrostic reflection follows. It acknowledges the importance of dignity, especially in the final months or days of a patient's life. I love the sentence about the dog. I know that many hospices encourage visits from pets, as well as fulfilling expressed wishes like going outside in the snow or meeting a famous person. One patient I heard about last year, was thrilled to see an actor he greatly admired coming into the hospice room. His widow now has the photo to cherish, an added bonus.

A very important aspect of dignity is coping with receiving help for personal tasks such as washing or agreeing to use a Zimmer frame or other aid. For some this seems like an infringement of dignity, but I, admittedly not having been in that situation, feel that dignity can be maintained by graciously accepting the need and maybe allowing a little humour in. Sensitivity of the staff and family can also enhance the sense of personal dignity.

D Dignity is central to us at the end of life
I Independence means the dog can visit
G God is only mentioned if the patient asks for her
N Night-time can be lonely, choices seem few
I Irredeemable - no not quite, but might seem so
T Time to graciously let others help you
Y Yes, it's tough, being yourself as the end draws near.

Section 6
Death and a rainbow

I have learnt much from a biography of Cicely Saunders. I was greatly moved as I read of her work and the thrust of her commitment and certitude towards vulnerable patients who could no longer be cured by traditional medicine. She was the catalyst for much appreciation of the value of every individual and the richness and potential of the time approaching death. Cicely Saunders talks of death as an achievement. 'In the right setting, with the right care, death could be an achievement; to accept death, when it was inevitable was not a negative thing to do'. It can be a time of reconciliation and spiritual depth. This is where we return to relationship again. It is a time when relationship to God comes into sharp focus, as well as relationships with other people, good and not so good, from the past.

'If we die with grateful hearts, our deaths can become sources of life for others.' Henri Nouwen

Brueggemann suggests that in facing difficult truths, we become stronger; we draw nearer to God and to one another.

One elderly lady, let's call her Martha, who died last year said that she was quite content and in good relations with everybody. She was a very committed Christian and quite a special lady - never a criticism of anyone.
There are others who are quite fearful of death. I know another person, let's call her Linda, who is terrified because she feels she has done many wrong things. She has a great sense of God as judge and forgets about his love and his mercy. If we feel like Linda, we would do well to remember God's promises of forgiveness - he will forgive us whatever we have done, and he asks us to forgive one another too.

My son texted me to ask what I was doing that day. With an older phone, I tried to type 'I'm burying a baby's ashes', but predictive texting had its way and the message came out 'I'm burying a baby's cries'. This was a moving mistake, but the meeting with the young parents and the burial was far more so. They showed me photos of their baby dressed up in smart blue clothes in the arms of each parent in turn. This was so important for them, this opportunity to say goodbye this way. I can't remember the family's name, but I remember that photobook and the love they showed this child, they saw him as beautiful, which was not at all how I, as an outsider, saw him.

This led to the following poem which was later published in 'Elements of Healing' by Poetry Space.

Ashes and Cries are much the same

According to predictive testing

I buried the baby's cry,
let the small white box
into the dark earth.
I buried his cries,
though they were silenced days before.

I buried his future,
his smiles and prattle,
the games he would play,
the words he would utter
dreams he would pursue.

I buried his name,
his address, his birthday,
his school reports,
his teacher's praise.

I tied them up in a blessing,
covered them with crumbling soil
and a carved stone.

There, his name will be chiselled,
refuse to be buried.

There, it will fill with the sky's tears
and glow in the warmth of the sun.

Feb 2012

The Memory Box

She paints your small, white foot
with vibrant vermillion,
then tenderly presses pure paper
against your near-perfect sole.
She holds it in place,
traces a loving finger over your heel,
and over your exquisite, pearly toes,
all five of them.

She places your footprint
into a nest of white tissue
beside three photos of you,
her studio son,
dolled up in tender blue knits,
held by Mum, Dad then Gran,
upright like the child you should be.

In her hand is your hospital
bracelet, tiny, with your
name and number.
Heart aching, she places
this memory of your life
beside the pictures
and the footprint.

She brushes your golden wisps
cuts them like corn,
arranges them on a small
blue card among forget-me-nots.
Through her tears, she can barely
see these fragile threads.

'He's beautiful' the nurse says,
I see your cracked, plaster skin,
your dull, unseeing eyes.

I watch with sadness,
knowing beauty is there
through the parents' eyes.

The nurse gives paints and brushes,
lets them freely swirl reds and blues
owed to you, in gracious curves,
images of love, of tear-filled gift -

I see a bird fly across the page.

This mother, Jenny, was a patient at the hospital and as her condition deteriorated, her only daughter struggled with a brain tumour. When Jenny was in hospital one time, a nurse brought her the news that Clare had died. She was concerned she would be too sick to attend the funeral. I am told that she did make it with much help.

Some weeks later, as I gather flowers for Jenny, I had no idea that it was Clare's birthday. I brought them to her bedside at home and it seemed as though I was bringing a gift for the birthday. Jenny's husband managed to find a vase, or was it a jam jar, and put the flowers near Jenny's bed.

Clare's birthday

Pink, yellow, white
(when will I learn their names?)
Still, I gather fine stems,
nodding heads, dropping bells,
capture them with love
embrace them with water
and a fine yellow wrap.

She lies in bed,
calm, solemn, accepting,
a flower pattern on her quilt.
As I offer the garden bunch,

she says, quizzically,
'It's Clare's birthday today',
(beloved daughter, who
died before her.) 'I can't
believe she's not here'.

The following story was told to me by a widow, and I tried to retell it in a way that befitted the moment. The widow, Sheila , was really touched by this retelling. Later I used it in a service for All Souls Day. One member of the congregation, a widower, came up to me and said that this story moved and helped him.

The Widow`s Rainbow

The widow sits,
numbed by tears.
Her prayers drift
round the grey church,
searching for God.
Her eyes dimly focus
on love-filled flowers,
on blurred images of friends
who smile kindly.
Words gently rumble past her
Songs tug at her grief.
The last amen sighs its farewell.

The people and the widow
leave the church.
She stands in sun-jewelled porch,
sees God in the sky,
a muted rainbow above the village.
She sees red, yellow and violet
arching over the dark figures
moving towards the gate.

I wrote this after the funeral service of an elderly musician, Fred. His great granddaughter played her cello and although the music came to an end it, like death itself, it seemed to sound on into the coming days.

Song from the Grave

Amen said;
cadence reaches death,
sounds silenced;
like the cold drop of winter,
firm covering of snow -
inert and bleak,
silent with farewell,
a lone word on a grave;

but music never dies;
new life rises from its chrysalis,
the song butterfly.

She sings,
true and tremulous,
stirs tears of grief
or is it joy?
squanders the spring air,
profligate, free,
with a new flight-bound sense of possibilities.

From the cross,
out of grief,
sing lilting notes,
death-warming, heart-lighting song -

yes,

butterfly song,

and laughter. 2004

Section 7
Grief and blossoms

I was asked to lead a writing group on bereavement in the cathedral as part of a conference.

I called it 'Finding a way to say it.' One woman wrote about life being like glass of wine that you sip and savour – she went on to liken it to a stilton cheese with blue veins running through it. The veins were pain, the world's and hers. The acknowledgement of those veins made the poem speak to the rest of us. Another poem spoke of a tear that might also be a bird.

For many people it is hard to face the reality of death. In our town there is a death café. This is a friendly happening where people can meet and speak openly about their feelings, about the partner who has died, or child, about their feelings towards their own death. They enjoy coffee and lovely cake and in this atmosphere of warmth and growing friendship, they can say just what they feel they need to say. Sometimes people will cross the road and not speak to a person recently bereaved as they don't know what to say. Sometimes people are afraid of grief, afraid of tears. They hesitate to mention the one who has died for fear of upsetting the bereaved person, when in fact all he wants is to talk about his wife. As those who have been bereaved recently know, that life's companion is never far from his or her mind and talking can be such a relief.

Writing too can help to explore and face all these feelings though it can be useful to have an understanding friend nearby, available for a hug or a coffee.

In the chapel where I worked for a number of years there is a book which contains the names of babies, beautifully written and kept under a glass cover. These are babies who have died; some of them died many years ago. They are remembered at a special service every July. Having an annual service with prayers, a talk and hymns is a great blessing to many parents. They return year after year and get to know and support one another

On the ward one day, a woman asked to speak to me. She wanted to talk about her baby who had died at birth some thirty years ago. That was before the acknowledgement that miscarriage and still birth have a shattering effect on parents. Meghan Markle has spoken publicly about their own experience of miscarriage in order to raise awareness of the reality which so many people do not acknowledge. The woman on the ward never knew what had happened to her baby. She never held him and was never given the opportunity to have some service of farewell. She didn't know where he was buried. On such occasions we can offer to have a service, to create a place where the parent can come to remember the child. I told her about the upcoming service for parents and families.

Nowadays these babies are remembered in a service which acknowledges the importance of this small life, this person whom they had begun to know in the womb. They are remembered before God who is the source of love and teaches us that all life is of value.

I was involved in a sad case where a young man died, and the parents did not approve of the girlfriend and refused to tell her when the burial and ceremony were to take place. Not surprisingly the story was more complicated than this. It was very sad, and everyone was hurting in their own way, unable to let others in. We arranged for a small service in our church for all the young man's friends. They spoke about him and what he meant to them. We planted a tree in his memory and for years, his girlfriend would come quietly to this spot, spend some time there and leave a token of her love.

The Memory Tree

In the corner of the plot
stands the memory tree;
it sighs,
broken by the world's neglect.

She comes in the silence;
she comes in the dusk,
stands by the memory stick,
hands full of tokens,
a rose, a trinket, a purse of hope.

With reverence in death,
pathos in the solitude,
She places the red and the blue
close to the cold earth.
Head bowed, maybe in prayer,
more likely in sorrow.

She pauses like a statue,
carved in time, moulded
by sadness, frozen in disbelief.
She pauses in her own silence,
then melts away,
soft steps on the evening grass.

This next poem details places of sanctuary and hope in a time of grief. Certain places can help us to grieve, places which are sacred or places which are beautiful or maybe resplendent with helpful memories.

Sanctuary

St. Mary offers me a ledge,
A perch beneath the scattered
windows' deep light,
gracious curves and a time to share.

St. Michael and all Saints give a blessing,
a hand of comfort, a drink,
a vast space with distant voices rumbling.

All Saints present me with a neat space,
a row of saints to share with,
an altar where bread has been broken.

Bishop Stanford lends me a tiny space,
full of colour,
refuge from bustle and preparation.
Light shines in, highlights a trio of saints.
A man bows his head in prayer.

I drink in the silence and the space.
I feast on the time that stands still.
I flourish on this diet of gracious light,
transcendental structures,
ancient solitude, muted prayer.

I walk away between the gravestones,
still bearing these gifts.
I nod to the past, the stone memories,
look to the future,
the stirring streets,
breathing poetry and conviviality.

2012

This poem follows a discussion about loss and bereavement. How would I or you respond? How have you responded?

When I am alone

When I am alone,
I'll beseech the mountain,
for wisdom and strength,
caress its burnished ridges,
aim for its peak against the sky.

When I am alone,
I'll woo the white swan.
trace his path across the gleaming lake,

retell the stories of this house,
revisit the bird hide
reopen our walk along the shore.

When I am alone,
I'll visit in the chapel,
clothe myself in words of comfort,
mouth prayers well-worn,
open my arms to the God of Sorrows.

Llangasty Retreat House, with a chapel.

This poem describes the character of the deceased, the person in all his vitality. It also acknowledges some of the strains that arise during a funeral. Family tensions can sometimes re-emerge at this time.

What you don't see

You disturb a buzzard
who scrambles from the tree.
On the stone, marred feathers,
blood, muddied bones.

Somewhere else a woman
and three men at a graveside.
Rain hiccups through the branches.
Roots disrupt the ragged grass.

A cavern opens to the frowning sky,
but it's not really a cavern, just
a small, neat oblong, ready for the
casket, her husband's ashes,

a small remnant of life; no
sign of smile, or of his wide
golf swing, no sound of his guffaw
emerging through his whiskers;

no glimpse of the Latin vespers
usually in his top pocket,
no sound of his deep voice,
reciting a Latin grace, no one understood.

The wooden box gravely announces
he was Charles Frederick Morris,
1942 – 2020.
The widow and sons shuffle and sniff,

ill at ease in each other's space.
Ill at ease in this windy church
yard, far from Margate.

A buzzard circles overhead.

The following poem highlights the value of sharing grief, of finding a person with time and care, ready to hear the story, or bits of it as they emerge. They may be fragmented. They may be very specific, like the scones and jam, but the telling creates a link with another person and gives value to the momentary outburst.

'I don't know what to say'

He stands with a black fire pot,
filled with orange blooms,
eyes cast down, shoulders hunched.
He stays by the small plot,
longing to speak to her.

In fact, he opens his mouth,
but nothing comes out.
He opens his heart,
a petal drops to the ground.
He opens his eyes,
a cloud gathers overhead.

He utters sounds, bleak
and meaningless, miserable
echoes of the tea-time chat,
last year. They hadn't said much
and yet they spoke with
smile, movement and sparkle,
blossom and colour.

Now he holds the colour to
his chest, petals wilting;
sees the damp grass, the cruel
blanket covering his wife.
There is no movement, no
sparkle, no touch or laughter.

He turns gently away,
and meets a stranger.
He tells her about the stutter,
the stammer, shows her the
pot of orange love,
tells her about the tea-time,

with the scones and red jam,
the sparkle and colour, the words
that slipped out so easily;
yes, she's still there somewhere
in his head, still orange and green,
still gold and purple,
all the colours of the rainbow.

The following tells of a grief so painful that other people in the parents' lives were shut out. They remained isolated for many years.

Sally

A photo hid in an old box.
- a holiday moment,
washed by the waves.
The girl smiled roundly,
The mother swam proudly.

Under the photo lay
a black-edged cremation notice.

Their life was a damaged photo.
They took scissors,
cut out all the faces,
sister's, nurse's, neighbour's,
friend's and God's –
cut out,
making holes with jagged edges,
spaces as black as crows' wings,
leaving just a mother and a father
and the ghost of a daughter.

Three in a frame,
in the crow-space of life.

The following poem explores the power of flowers and words, the multiple meanings behind them and the memories they evoke.

Flowers and Words

They will lie on the coffin,
words between petals
wishes hidden among the smells,
words for our father, words for the day.
printed in Times New Roman,
on a card, not chosen by us.
placed in the space between life and death,
between body and ash.

Perhaps they're a prayer.
Maybe God will read them.

The words were chosen
by my sister; she
picked them like flowers,
texted me her thoughts.

They resonate with memories of
shared seats in the car,
shared toothpaste tubes.
pots of porridge,
fanfares of Beethoven.
in the room with the flowered carpet.

They're a prayer from us all.
God will read them.

Section 8

Peace through prayers

the hungry people
who fear annihilation.

She hears the flight of a bomb.
She fears its hideous explosion.
She flees with her frightened brother.

The first words I dare to spell out
are an answer to her stare,
as she looks at the world this morning

glint-eyed
sure,
far away.

Syria

T torn edges, broken names

E elbow into history's tome.

A after destruction, collapse,

R ruined city, splintered lives.

Acrostic of TEAR, which might mean tearing, as in the torn edges, it also has overtones of tears, which we spill when moved or upset.
This short piece leads us into another story from Syria.

This is a story told by my daughter, who worked for the church in Istanbul with refugees, some from Syria and some from Africa. She was the woman, who was able to have Yousef's hearing aid repaired. To raise the money, she shared the story on Facebook and many friends from around the world donated to this fund.

Now I offer you a variety of prayers and reflections that may act as a resource for personal or public use.

Psalm 139

O Lord you search me and you know me,
you know my resting and my rising.
You know my frailty and my frustrations.
You know my tears and my inward musings.

O Lord you discern my purpose from afar.
Guide my praying and my longing.
Guide my listening and acknowledging.

O Lord you search me and you know me,
You know my resting and my rising.
O Lord you know my weakness and my emptiness.
You know my waiting and my yearning.

Guide my waiting and my musings.
Inhabit my waiting and my musings,
that I may wait for you
and long for your kingdom on earth as it is in heaven.

Peace in the Silence

Prayer, place, powerlessness,
Emptying, unwinding, waiting,
Aching, actively hunting,
Craning, caressing, careful,
Emptying, energising, ever hopeful.

Peace becomes prayer…

Piercing cry, pandemonium,
Reaching outwards, stretching,
Aiming for God, arching, aching,
Yearning for angels, stars, dewdrops,
Earthing hopes, grounding dreams,
Realising riches, counting blessings.

Be Still and Know that I am God

Ruffled by the turmoil of the day,
tossed by the storms and winds,
sing God's quiet refrain -
Be still and know that I am God

Be still; let go - leave pain and pleasure behind you
Be still; give God the ruffled, white-tipped waves.
Be still; hand her the small gusts of wind.
Be still; touch the stars and the depths of this dark night
Be still; and rest.

Be still
and know that I am God; feel the strength of my anchor
know that I am God; listen to the music of the waves
that I am God; drink deeply of the wine of love
I am God; rest assured on the calm sea.

As you hear the music of love,
be still and know that I am God

Prayer for balance

O Source of life and comfort,
giver of life, movement,
warmth and action,
teach me how to be,
when to do,
when to embrace
and when to withdraw,

how to act and when to breath,
how to focus and when to sigh,
how to plan and when to pray,
how to stand still and when to laugh.

When we feel sad or dispirited it can be helpful to look into ourselves and explore what lies beneath this feeling. Sometimes it is clear but at other times it may be complex or puzzling. This poem expresses this exploration.

The Wisdom of Sad

I spoke to Sad,
looked into her eye's heart,
deeply, as into the pond's pit.
Who are you? I asked
What are the sum of your parts?
Spell your name, or your many names.

Slowly she returned my gaze.
She listed three or four items,
looking deep into my soul
through the magnifying glass
over the gate
along the lane.

Each name she spoke cleared my heart.
The tumble weed, crossed wires,
the deadened dance.
Each called from her unfazed
open-mouthed honesty.

By the end
I knew her names,
the reed beds, the crossroads
the liquid mirage,
all told me who she was.

'Thank you, Sad', I mouthed
'thank you' I whispered,
'thank you' I cried.
Now I know your names.

I can turn onwards,
walk through the turnstile of tomorrow

Trinity of Love

God of Compassion surround me and hold me,
Son of Healing anoint me, soothe my way,
Spirit of Comfort strengthen and uphold me.

Trinity of relationship, hold hands around me,
include me in your loving,
say my name in your streets,
write my needs in your pages,
catch my tears in your cup.

Trinity of hope, pour your grace into my life,
that I may receive it and respond;
open my arms to embrace it;
open my heart and let it settle like snow;

Let me know I am yours,
as I pause in my life's journey,
as I look at the signposts,
the map of the road ahead.

God of Compassion surround me and hold me,
Son of Healing anoint me, soothe my way,

Section 9

Invitation to play with words

Writing can help us to let go of overwhelming emotions. It can help us to explore ideas. It can also be fun and gives us a chance to play. Please do not worry whether it is 'good enough'. If you enjoy it, if it helps you, it is certainly good enough.

I suggest that, when you try any of these exercises you are writing for yourself. There are no rules, except that you write what you need to write. You can change the exercises. This should be your time and space. Grammar, spelling and form are not important when you do this. You need to take responsibility for what you write, in the sense that you need to be aware of the impact of exploring a powerful subject. Is it wise to tackle a painful subject today? Have you got anyone to turn to if you find yourself upset?

Here are some ideas.

Peace acrostic – start a sentence with each of these letters in turn.

P
E
A
C
E

For example: -

Stillness Acrostic

Slowly welcome the day.
Take time to honour its beauty.
Irrigate the flowers with love.
Look into the eyes of a fox.
Linger with the words of the day.
kNeel in the chapel of peace.
Explore the gifts of the day.
Succour the sweetness on offer.
Search for things of God.
Sow seeds to enrich the garden.
'Be still and know that I am God.'

Choose a sentence from a poem that inspires you and write it down and carry on with what you want to say.

Here are some sentences that you might like to work with –

Love changes everything…
Be near me when the light is Low… Tennyson
The wintry winds have ceased to blow… George Crabbe
When I feel overwhelmed by destruction, let me go down to the sea… Marjorie Pizer
Time does not heal, it makes a half-stitched scar… Elizabeth Jennings

Draw the shape of a leaf, a cross or tear (if you're up to it). Fill your shape with words that come into your head. You might include some images? Or you might write around the outside of the shape. You might want to draw your scar and decorate it or surround it with words.

Choose an object that speaks to you of someone you love and miss. (Only start on this one if you are feeling strong). It might be a shoe or an umbrella or a bicycle wheel. It could be an object that is important to you.

Tell your story. Write about what has been happening to you.

What does it feel like to be really carefully listened to? 'When you listen deeply to me…' continue this train of thought. [12]

Write a letter to God. Be honest, he can take it.

Write an answer from God.

Friendship

What are fragile? Buttercups and beauty
What are serene? Saints and sunshine.
What are fiery? Storms and fury.
What are enduring? Fossils and friendship.

Take these four questions and find your own answers. You might choose a different theme

Here is a haiku, a poem of 17 syllables, arranged in lines of 5,7 and 5. Traditionally the last line is a change of direction, something of a surprise. Try writing a haiku about your experience.

I pick up a seed
plant it, water it, watch it;
it tells my story.

What will you do with your writing? Share it with someone close to you or with your spiritual director, if you have one? Put it in a special, safe place? Put it on one side to add to or rewrite one day? You might have other ideas.

Section 10
Playground

Here is some space for you to play, play with words and images, find what you need to say.

Judy comes from Colchester, from a musical family. She has taught languages, worked as a hospital social worker and is an ordained priest. She has an MA in creative writing. She married John, a doctor, and they have three children and seven grandchildren. Judy has always worked with people: children, neighbourhood groups, patients and parishioners. During lockdown, she gathered poems written as hospital chaplain and began to create this book. The poems are vignettes of peoples' lives, little stories that caught her attention over many years. Other stories crept into the book which shed light on issues faced by many patients.

Judy wrote stories as a child and, with inspiration from the Christian Iona Community on Scotland's beautiful island, later discovered the joy and value of writing poetry. She writes for Wild Goose, the Iona publishers and has also been published in anthologies and magazines. Judy runs creative writing workshops with neighbourhood groups, schoolchildren and colleagues. Leading retreats is another way she uses poetry. They give participants space to explore issues, often in delightful venues.

Judy is grateful to her family for their support, to Mark Oakley for valuable advice and to Susan Jane Sims, her helpful and patient editor.

Poems previously published:

'Widow's Rainbow' – Triumph House 1996

'Carol Ann' - Housman Society competition, published by The Housman Society 2000

'Christ you take care of our illness' 'Psalm 139'

Lifting Women's Voices, Moorhouse Publishing, New York 2009

'Ashes and Cries', 'Purple Smile' - Elements of Healing, Poetry Space 2010

'Helen' – Saying Goodbye, Wild goose Publishing ed Ruth Burgess 2013

'Emma' and 'Martha Jones' - Spotlights Paragram 2015

'Trudge of Exile' - 'A Scream of Many Colours' , Poetry Space, 2016

'Five Gifts' -Poetry Space website: 2017

'George' - Poetry Space Summer Showcase. 2018

'Sparkle and Blooms' – Poetry Space Showcase, Spring 2019

'Below the water lily' – Locked Down, poetry, diary extracts and art from the 2020 pandemic , Poetry Space, 2021.

Endnotes

1. *Page 9:* Nouwen, Henri , 'Life of the Beloved', The Crossroad Publishing Company, New York, 2002.

2. *Page 24:* Silf, Margaret, 'At Sea with God' Darton, Longman & Todd Ltd, 2003.

3. *Page 34*: Burgess, Ruth (ed.) 'A Book of Blessings and How to Write your Own', Wild Goose Publications, 2004.

4. *Page 37:* Mannix, Kathryn 'With the End in Mind' William Collins, 2018.

5. *Page 39*: MacQuarrie, John, 'Principles of Christian Theology', SCM Press, 1966 p. 497.

6. *Page 39*: Rohr, Richard 'Daily Reflections', February 2021.

7. *Page 42:* Moltmann, Jürgen 'In the End – the Beginning', SCM Press.

8. *Page 65:* Selby, Peter, 'Rescue' SPCK,1995.

9. *Page 68:* Clark, David, 'Cicely Saunders: A Life and Legacy' - OUP, USA, 2018.

10. *Page 69:* Sims, Mark, PS I have Cancer: wrestling melanoma and falling in love, Poetry Space Ltd 2018 and Sims, Susan Jane 'Splitting Sunlight', Dempsey & Windle, 2018 .

11. *Page 76*: Mayne, Michael, 'A Year Lost and Found' Dalton, Longman & Todd, 1987.

12. *Page 107:* Bolton, Gillie, 'Writing Works': A Resource Handbook for Therapeutic Writing Workshops and Activities', Jessica Kingsley Press, 2006.

Other Resources

Autton, Canon Norman, 'Sick Visiting, Mowbray: London & Oxford.

Cotter, Jim 'By Stony Paths': A Version of Psalms 51-100, Cairns Publications 1991.

Eadie, Donald, 'Grain in Winter' (Unavailable).

McClement, Susan E. 'Spiritual issues in palliative medicine', 2015 Oxford. University Press.